Podcasting for Dollars

How to Create & Grow Your Own Internet Talk Show

By Sam Raiden

About This Book

Have you ever listened to a podcast on iTunes or elsewhere and thought, "I can do that"? The truth is, you could do that. It's much easier than you might imagine. A successful podcast can easily reach many thousands and thousands of people (sometimes hundreds of thousands) and is an incredible way on which to build a business or augment an existing one.

You can create a podcast on almost any topic...and have it to be successful. The Internet is a very, very large place and if your podcast is well-designed, you will attract a large audience. Perhaps your interest is in politics, religion, business, health, or even a hobby such as fine wine, you can easily create a podcast on that topic...and make money from home.

Podcasting for Dollars takes you through the process of selecting the right equipment and software, setting it up, and making it go in your first podcast. You'll learn how to market your podcast, how to gain followers, and how to make money from your podcast. It's much easier than you could ever imagine which is why the industry is growing so quickly.

In this book, you will learn

- what is the best kind of microphone for your podcast
- what kind of computer you would need for your podcast
- the best recording software for your podcast
- how to create an RSS feed for your podcast
- where to upload your podcast for maximum exposure

- how to earn money from your podcast
- and much more

Radio is dead and the future is here... and it's podcasting

Table of content

Copyright Notice

Dedicated to the owners of all those strange and mysterious voices
on the AM band that I used to listen to as a young child late, late at night..

...and just remember,

"Argue for your limitations, and sure enough they're yours."
- Richard Bach

Introduction

I am sure that this is by no means the first time you are hearing of the word podcasting. If you have been around for a bit (i.e. assuming you are not below teenage), you have at one point of the other listened to a podcast, either knowingly or unknowingly. If we were to step into a time machine and go back a couple of years when the internet was the new kid on the block, we would see that the free and liberal internet we have today is a towering master of the internet shadow that was. Are you wondering how this relates to podcasting for either fun or money? Well, in the early and not so early days of the web and content development, search engine optimization, and online money, very few options of making money online were available to 'netpreneurs'. Today, that has changed, a lot.

While the traditional ways of making money such as blogging are still viable today, and still look viable in the near future, internet marketers and internet enthusiasts are always on the lookout for new and better ways to make money or interact with their followers or the millions of people using technology to learn new and exciting stuff. While podcasting is not new per se, more and more people are coming to the realization that not only is podcasting a good way to make some money, it is also an ideal way to create and cement a personal relationship between the person listening to the podcast and the one making the podcast. This is the best time to get started in podcasting. If you are new to podcasting and want to master the ins and outs of podcasting, this book will help you get started. There is a lot to learn so let's get started.

Understanding Podcasting and How It Works

As I indicated earlier, I am sure that this is not your first contact with the term 'podcast' or podcasting. However, it may come as a surprise to many people to learn that despite being a popular word, very few people have the true meaning of what podcasting is or how it works.

Technically, a podcast is a digital, RSS 2.0 feed downloadable file. The media file of a podcast can be any type. Essentially, sharing a podcast requires the web address of the media file to be included in the RSS feed in an enclosure tag of an XML file. While I said that a podcast media file could be of any type, it is important to note that most of the aggregators identify and play specific media files only. In most cases and more often than not, a podcast is an audio, video or both. A podcast may sound like an online streaming radio but is indeed not. For one, a podcast is a non-streamed audio or video, which means, you do not watch the files online; instead, you download them and watch or listen to them on your mp3 player, smartphone, or video player. Podcasts are often times free (unless the creator states a buying price). Essentially, a podcast allows you to get a variety of songs and video that you can download to your player and listen at your convenience. Another not-so-complicated way of looking at podcasting or a podcast is to imagine it as your own personal radio channel or radio station on a mobile device or mp3 player. The fun thing about a podcast and in extension podcasting is that you do not need a broadcasting degree to do it. With technology all around us, anyone, including you, can create and publish a podcast on the internet in a matter of minutes, literally.

If you have been keen with everything so far, you may be wondering if there is a difference between a podcast and downloading music or videos from the many sites available on the internet. There is a difference, a very big one. While you may be required to push a few buttons on your keyboard and a few clicks on your mouse to download a video or audio music, getting a new podcast is not so overly complicated. When a user subscribes to a podcast, they need not do anything else. Any new podcast published on that channel will automatically be synchronized with all connected devices. Essentially, all you need to receive a podcast and future podcasts from a specific podcast is to subscribe to that specific podcast and everything else happens automatically.

You may also be curious about how podcasting works. Let me explain how it works.

How podcasting works

As earlier indicated, podcasts go through an RSS 2.0 feed. The owner of the podcast embeds the file in the RSS feed and uploads it to a podcasting website. The embedded RSS feed contains the URL for the media file (video or audio), and whenever a new user subscribes to the podcast, they automatically get the latest podcast. For any user to subscribe to a podcasting service, they require a podcast aggregator, or podcatcher software. Using the software, a user can subscribe to any podcast service. The software then regularly checks for feeds and podcast updates just like a normal RSS reader would.

With that in mind, you may be wondering why you should even think of trying podcasting in the first place. Just to give you some motivation to get started, let's discuss why you should try podcasting.

Reasons Why You Should Create a Podcast

For a minute, think of traditional media as a tether holding back your creativity and explosively intuitive voice and advice. Now, without vacating this frame of mind, think of podcasting as an Old West, sharp, shaving knife or a pair of sharp scissor cutting the tether, letting your imagination roam free, and letting your vocal and video ideas and talents burst at the seams. Podcasting is the medium you need to share your creativity, thoughts, opinions, advice, music and whatever else you can create be it for fun or for some money. Podcasting offers you and other podcasters limitless possibilities to express yourself and voice your ideas and opinions. Podcasting allows you to host your very own show or promote products and services. Further, podcasting can give you a platform to give your expertise a voice for more and better recognition in your field of work or study. This coupled with the fact that podcasting is a fun way to interact and connect with other people forms part of the reason why you should care about podcasting. As topping on the above reasons, here are seven more reasons why you should create your own podcast.

Ease of use

Before you get the opportunity to host a radio or TV program on any network, you have to undergo thousands of hours in training as a journalist or as presenter. In fact, not everyone that trains in that field gets the opportunity to be a radio or TV host. Podcasting is utterly different from this. To get started with your first podcast, all you need is a working computer, a working microphone (even the inbuilt microphone on computers will work), and an internet connection. In truth, these items are all you need to get started on your first podcast. This does not mean that the podcast will be great or turn heads, but the fact remains that it will still be a podcast despite its poor quality. As you get better and confident in creating podcasts, you can then move on to expensive and better quality gear. In broadcasting, both TV and radio, you have to contend with FCC regulations and expenses in broadcasting. Podcasting cuts all this out and gives you an easy and direct link to the target audience. This brings me to my second point.

A focused audience in record time

By choosing your content and podcast subject wisely, you can get a huge following and listener crowd very fast. This is not all. While radio and TV stations are geo-location locked, a podcast is not. This simply means that with the right content, you can get a worldwide audience in very little time. What this spells for a business or a global citizen is the added advantage of either growing your customer base or audience. One main reason why podcasting holds some advantage over traditional broadcasting is its targeted listening. What does this mean? It means that while a radio or TV channel broadcasts to a wide demographic of individuals, some who do not give a hoot about the content broadcasting on the said channel, a podcast lets you target specific demographics. For example, if you have a stamp collection hobby, and would like to create a podcast for stamp collection enthusiasts, you are leaving nothing to chance. Anyone who downloads or subscribes to your podcast is already a stamp collection enthusiast. Therefore, your work is not to interest them in stamp collection, but to give them sound advice or entertainment with content that would tickle a stamp collector. This then makes podcasting a very effective tool for self and product promotion.

Total and complete control

Compared to normal broadcasting where a personality is online at a specified time, podcasting is not so restrictive. With podcasting, you have complete control over your podcast and podcasting career. You decide when and how often you record and distribute your podcasts. Further, depending on your distribution channel, podcasting is not restrictive in terms of formats. Podcasting gives you total and complete control over your podcasting activities. You can podcast from the comfort of your home, a bar, a boat and anywhere else provided that the audio or video is audible. Further, no one dictates the theme or content of your podcast. In fact, your worst enemy in podcasting is simply your imagination. However, it is important to note that copyright laws also apply to podcasting. Therefore, you cannot use other people's content as your own without their consent.

Convenient, cheap, and automatic

When someone subscribes to your podcast that is all they need to do. Any other content you create or add to the podcast will automatically go to their preferred device. Automation is the major reason why podcasting has become so popular. Further, the convenience this offers you and your audience is immeasurable. In terms of cost, unless you intend to be a pro podcaster, there is no reason why podcasting should cost you an arm and a leg. It may be wise to invest in some equipment to ensure quality podcasts. However, this is not mandatory.

Human connection

If you are a blogger, and even if you are not, you know that as humans, we crave a human connection. Compared to blogs and articles on your website or blog, a podcast is personal. Since the beginning of time, the human voice is a tool humans use to communicate in a way words cannot begin to comprehend or compare. When people listen to your podcast, they can feel your presence. It is easy for them to imagine that you are right there in the room with them teaching them what you know.

This helps cement the human connection between a listener and the person podcasting. This is not only essential in building a lasting relationship; it also guarantees the podcaster a loyal audience who become loyal fans. What this then means is that podcasting is not only fun, it is also a powerful way of connecting with your audience and delivering your message to them.

Recognition as an expert or trendsetter on a specific niche

If you are passionate about something that you think the masses will like, a podcast is the cheapest, quickest, and ideal way to stamp your authority on that subject. For example, if you have a passion for stamps, and have been collecting them for the last, say 30 years, you are an expert in the field of stamp collection. By using a podcast, you can get recognition due to your vast expertise in that field.

Podcasting has no restriction to which field you can be an expert. If you passionate about partying and would like to be an expert in the field, with podcasting, you are free to explore that stream. Podcasting is a new frontier. What do I mean? Let me give you an example. You are an expert in acne blogging, you may not be the only one. However, you may be the first one to create 'how to effectively deal with acne' podcast. This means that not only are you stamping your authority, you are also creating a new niche for your fans and followers. This then translates to recognition from your fans, who will always turn to you or your podcast for advice, and from industry leaders who will want to reach out to you for product placements.

Make money

It has taken a while but we are finally reached the part you have been waiting for. Yes, podcasting is a viable way of making money especially now that people are turning to podcasts for advice. People are always on the look out for valuable information and are always eager to pay any amount of money for helpful information. For example, if you offer sound acne advice for the millions of people suffering from it, you can bet that most of them would be willing to pay for that information if the information is actionable.

I hope the above reasons have stirred your interest and you are now ready to get started in creating your first podcast. Podcasting for the complete beginner has four stages. Each of these stages is very essential in creating a vibrant and informational podcast. To make the learning process easy learn, we shall look at these four stages in chapter-by-chapter form.

Getting Started- Preparing For Your First Podcast

As I indicated earlier, podcasting is more popular now than it was several years ago. If you are ready to create your first podcast, let us begin. Again, as indicated earlier, we shall look at the four stages of podcasting in chapter form. The first step is preparation. Preparing for your first podcasts comes even before you click on the record button on your equipment or computer. We can break preparing for your podcast into three steps. Let us look at these steps.

Step one: Determining the nature and subject of your podcast

As I said earlier, podcasting is not as restrictive as traditional broadcasting. However, this does not mean that it is a walk in the park either. Deciding the content of your podcast is one of the most important decisions you will make in your podcasting career regardless of your reason for podcasting (money or just for fun). Brainstorm some ideas of what will be the main contents of your podcasts and write the ideas down. I must point out that podcasts are more or less like episodes. One episode has to be a continuation of the last episode or building on concepts built in the last episode. Write down your ideas and create a sort of roadmap for your talking and discussion points.

The list of topics you can cover is endless. For example, podcast.com, a podcast distribution, lists podcasts on the platform by category. There are many categories including news, music, health, comedy, Harry Potter book and many more.

My advice is to choose a few of the more popular podcasts and listen to them just to get a feel of how the pros are doing it. Use this to draft up your ideas list and podcasting approach.

If you have a target audience for your podcast, it also would not hurt to do some research into what types of topics would interest that demographic and how they would expect you to present the information you have to offer. More importantly, make sure that you write everything you intend to talk about on the podcast. This part is very important because it eliminates the awkward silences and pauses in between your podcast.

Here are tips on how to choose a topic or subject for your podcast

Tips on how to choose what topic to podcast about

Tip one: Answer the 'why' question

Why do you want to broadcast your podcast? What do you aim to get from it? Are you doing it for fun or for some money? It is wise to ask yourself the why question in terms of the people who will subscribe to your podcast. The audience, or rather, potential audience, will also be struggling with the why question. Why should I trust you? Why should I subscribe to your podcast?

When you define your why i.e. why you are doing a podcast, it will form the backbone for your motivation and interest in your preferred subject. Further, you should note that in podcasting, the money motivation is simply inadequate. Set a smart goal for your why. Determining your why will also play a very big role in helping you create content that answers the subscribers' why questions?

Tip Two: What is entertaining and or helpful?

Podcasting is a personal connection between the subscribers and the podcaster. Before someone can subscribe to your channel, he or she is looking for one of these two things: entertainment or information. Information could mean information that helps the listener take some action in a specific area of their life. For example, a podcast about how to make stock investments is helpful so is any podcast on the many how to subjects. On the other hand, an entertainment podcast could be making people laugh, inspiring them, or driving their interest. For example, a comic podcast (a podcast centered on jokes) may be entertaining and so is a music podcast. When you decide which subject to pursue on your podcast, you will easily know what is entertaining or informative.

Tip Three: Follow your passion

Whichever topic you zero in on, ensure that you are passionate about it. Passion is what drives you to create more podcasts even when you have zero subscribers. Moreover, it is important to point out that in the beginning, you will have zero subscribers. Passion for a specific subject also shines through in the way you talk about it. If you are not passionate about a subject and are doing it for the money, you can bet that this will reflect in the quality of your podcast. Not in terms of sound quality, but in terms of topic and content quality. By picking a subject of interest to you, you enthusiastically pursue the subject and communicate that enthusiasm to the subscribers.

Tip Four: What is relevant to you why?

What is relevant to your audience? What are they looking to get out of the podcasts you create? What would make them happier to learn? For example, while you may decide to create a podcast about dealing with acne, it would be more relevant to create a podcast about 'dealing with acne the natural way'. Why? Because someone suffering from acne may have tried most 'acne health care products' with little or no success.

Tip Five: Consider your expertise on that subject of field

In truth, podcasting is more about your courage, boldness, and audacity to broadcast than it is about your skills. However, this does not entail a pass to have lousy content on your podcast. A podcast is verbal, visual, and at times, both. While your subject and content may be great, you still need to do one more thing to make the podcast stand out among many others i.e. present it. Not just present it, but also present it succinctly and in an understandable manner. You must have the knowledge to produce and edit the audio or video clip well, convert it into another media file if necessary, and use the internet to upload it. Fortunately, you do not have to be an expert in a specific field; if you are passionate about it, you can start now and learn along the way and share that journey with those who subscribe to your podcast.

Step Two: Choose your podcasting equipment and products

Creating a podcast is easy. In fact, you can create a podcast by using the microphone on your laptop or PC. However, the microphone on your laptop or PC is at best, iffy. This means that your podcast will be of low quality. In podcasting, quality takes precedence. Therefore, you need to invest some of your time and money into finding equipment and products you can use to create your podcast. This may include buying a new noise cancelation headset with microphone, a mixer if you are using an analog microphone, and even a new computer. Do not; I repeat, DO NOT, make the mistake of assuming that the microphone on your computer is capable of recording quality sound especially if you have an intention of sounding or coming of as a pro in your podcast. You can get affordable sound recording equipment online or at your local music store.

You also need to consider one other thing of vital importance: where will you podcast from, will you podcast from home or on the go? If your podcast location will be home, it is ok to invest in some non-portable equipment. However, if your podcast will be on the go, having non-portable equipment is not feasible or logical. Therefore, you may need to invest in a smartphone or a portable voice-recording device

Tips For Choosing Podcasting Equipment

Tip One: Pick you microphone carefully

A microphone is the mouthpiece you will use to communicate with your podcast community. If you have a terrible mic, your sound will come out in gurgles or hardly audible. Remember that except in video podcasts, the only connection between you and the person listening to the podcast is your voice. If your voice is inaudible in one podcast, not only does it spell 'unprofessional', the audience will be quick to click on the unsubscribe button.

Tip Two: Choose your location well

Sometimes, it is possible to choose your recording location, at other times, not so much. I cannot offer you much advice in terms of the best location for creating your podcast; all I can say is that location is important. If you are creating the podcast at home or indoors, you should choose a room that does not bounce sound off the wall i.e. a room that has some carpeting and items on the wall. If your podcast is on the go, try as much as you can to avoid recording your podcast in noisy environments. Essentially, you can record your podcast anywhere, in the car, bathroom, or closet. The key point is to make sure that the location is noise and distraction free.

Tip Three: Carefully choose your video camera

If you are recording a video podcast, a good camera is essential. In video, you have many choices, the easiest and most productive one being a digital camera; well, it is best to opt for a DSLR if you really want high quality videos. This is because if you decide to use an analog camera, you will have to go through the process of converting that video into a digital format. A good, simple, but clear camera is adequate for podcasting purposes.

Step Three: Choose your recording software

There are a ton of recording software on the web and other software market places. Choose a recording software depending on your operating system. If you are on OSX, you can use the GaragBand, which comes in the out of the box version of OSX as part of the iLife suite. If you are on Windows, you can use the voice recorder. Further, there are many other free recording software such as Audacity that offer great audio recording. If you are also feeling up to it, you may decide to go with a paid recording software such as Sony Acid or Music Studio.

Alternatively, you can use industrial Audio Software's such as iPodcast producer that are very podcast friendly and helpful in the recording of the podcast all through to uploading the finished podcast. Most of the commercial audio recording software are not free.

Choose a software depending on your knowledge in its use, budget, and the software's ease of use. The interface is also something you should consider. I have found that some software are relatively easy to use and very powerful if you can circumnavigate their complicated interfaces.

Five things you must consider and have before you hit record

Before we move on to the second part of our podcasting journey, I think and feel it is only right to point out some things you may be tempted to overlook while preparing for your first podcast. I will keep it short and brief.

One: The title of your podcast

Your podcast show cannot thrive without a title. If you have a blog or brand name, that would be the most logical choice for your title. However, you also have the opportunity to add some flair to the title rather than simply giving it your blog or brand name. Further, you should note that your title is searchable by search engine which means your title should also be search engine friendly. Yes, iTunes (if that is where you intend to upload your podcast), is also a search engine.

Two: Your Talent/Host name

Your talent name should often be your name. Nevertheless, this does not mean that you should shy away from adding something more after the name to help you in ranking higher in podcast market places such as iTunes.

Three: Subtitle for your podcast

Most podcast directories will ask for a subtitle for your show. While it may not make much sense to have a subtitle, especially because most of the platforms do not show the subtitle, it does not hurt to have one either. Ensure that it has some keywords in it and an apt description of your show.

Four: A summary and description for your podcast

A description for your show should come the moment you decide which topic you aim to discuss on your show. If you aim to upload to iTunes, you have 4000 characters for the description. The description should be in copy form i.e. it should be descriptive, engaging and captivating. Furthermore, you should also throw in some keywords in there for good measure.

Five: Artwork for your podcast

Your podcast is an audio file. Therefore, it will need an album art. An album artwork is a square image that is a representation of your show. Think of it in terms of a book cover. Artwork is important because it is what people will see in podcast directories before they even make the choice to subscribe to your channel. Your artwork is also the image someone listening to your podcast on his or her mp3 player will see. Most album arts are 1400 x 1400 pixels and in .jpg or .png format

With the above ready and out of the way, we are ready to jump into the exciting part of our podcast, which is recording. In the next chapter, we shall look at exactly that.

Creating and Recording Your Podcast

Are you excited? I am. This is simply the most exciting part of podcasting. With all the rigorous preparations we have undertaken, it is time to put everything into action.

To begin, you need to prepare your content further. This entails putting together some form of script to direct what you will say at the start of the podcast and how you transition from topic to topic. Make content that is easy to read and follow down the list. Here is a sample content preparation list you can follow.

#- Intro the show- Use this to introduce yourself and the topic you will be discussing. Keep it under a minute.

#- An intro jingle or music- consistently use one jiggle or song so that listeners can associate that music with your show. Also, keep it below a minute

#- Discuss topic one for 3 minutes

#- Discuss topic two for 3 minutes

#- A 30-second interlude with music

#- Discuss topic three for 3minutes

#- Discuss topic four for 3 minutes

#- A two minutes closing remark where you thank the guest, audience and give insight into the next show

#- Closing music preferably the same as the intro music for 2 minutes.

Whatever format you opt for, make sure that it is easy to follow from beginning to end. Also, make sure that the topics in the above format are interesting. You should also note that this does not mean you should have a new topic every few minutes. You can have the same topic only from a different perspective.

With that in mind, you are ready to record the audio for your podcast. At this point, your podcasting is at a critical juncture and if you fail to do this properly, you will probably end up repeating the process several times (the truth is that you will repeat the process several times before you get it right). The trick to recording good podcasts is to keep your podcast friendly, conversational, and talking in a consistent pace. This is where you let passion for the topic in discussion shine through. Follow the script you created, but do not be afraid to improvise if the situation calls for it. As indicated, it may take a couple practice runs before you can commence recording the actual podcast you will upload. Again, let your passion drive you and do not quit. I have also found it necessary to take the software and the equipment for test runs by recording samples, listening to them, and adjusting my equipment and software.

If your podcast does involve other people ('a podcast party') by far, the easiest way to record this is by employing Skype call recorder. You can use Skype to call the guests then record the call via special Skype recording software. You can then use an editing software to edit and clean the audio. If you are on OSX, you can record Skype calls with call recorder for Skype and edit it in GarageBand. In addition, if you are on Windows, you can record Skype call using Pamela and edit them with Audacity

Preparing the audio file

After recording your audio file, you need to save it. You can save the file in a folder of your choice on your computer. More importantly, you should save the file in mp3 format with a bit rate of 128kbps and 192 if you feature any music. This means that if your recording is in .wav, you need to convert it into mp3 using an audio conversion software.

When saving your file, avoid using special characters such as @, # or % in the file name. After saving, open your media players and listen to the entire audio clip. Take notes of the areas that need some editing and once you are through with this, open up your sound editor and edit the audio. Edit out background noises and cut out any long pauses in the audio. Add your intro, interlude, and closing music.

Note: It is very important and critical that you save a backup of your raw audio file before you begin editing. This is to make sure that in case there is some sort of mishap; you have a backup that you can fall back on.

After editing your music, listening to it and making sure that there are no mistakes in the file, you can now tag it. Tagging your file means adding author information, artist information, genre, and adding an album art. If you do not have an album art, you can outsource the work to freelance graphic designers or find copyright free images online. Because the audio is in the final production stages, take careful note of how you name the file. You want a name that is relevant to the topic in discussion and your podcast. You may also want to add a production date and edit the ID3 tags.

Creating an RSS feed for your podcast

At the beginning of this book, I indicated that a podcast is a downloadable RSS 2.0 file. Your feed must meet the industry standard for an authentic 2.0 feed with enclosures. You can use a professional service such as Libsyn, Podomatic, or Castmate to create your RSS feed. However, you should note that if you have longer podcasts, you might have to pay a fee.

In my view, the easiest way to create your RSS feed is by using a blog. If you do not already have a blog on the major platforms i.e. blogger, WordPress, and the other blogging service, you can create one by heading over to their respective homepages. Make sure that your blogpost title matches that of your podcast title. You do not have to create any new posts just yet. Essentially, a feed is a container for the audio file. It tells aggregator programs where to search for new podcast episodes. If you are feeling up to it, you can create an RSS feed manually using XML coding. However, the internet is overflowing with other much simpler methods of creating an RSS feed for your podcast. This one here is the best option available.

After creating your RSS 2.0 feed, you are ready to upload your file to the various podcast platforms and aggregators. This is what we shall look at in the next chapter.

Uploading and Marketing Your Podcast

Uploading your podcast will largely depend on the platform you intend to use. However, you still need to get your feed on the internet. Start by going to FeedBurner and typing in your web URL (even the URL to your blog post will do). Once you enter this, click on the "I am a podcaster" option on the next screen. Go ahead and configure all the elements of your podcast (any information relative to your podcast). Once you create a FeedBurner feed, it becomes your podcast.

After creating this, you can then go to one of the many hosts available online and signup. Go to your files and upload your mp3 file. Head over to your blog or website and create a new blog post with the same title as the podcast. This is important because the content of this post will show up on the show notes or description option of the feed. After writing the post on your blog or website, put a link to the media file at the tail end of the post.

Be patient; within a few minutes, FeedBurner will add this to your feed after which you are good to go! You have an episode that you can submit to podcast directories such as iTunes.

There is no art to submitting your podcast to podcast directories. For example, on iTunes, the podcast page has mega button that requests for the RSS link and additional information about your podcast. Do not forget to include a subscription button on your website to inform people about subscribing to your podcast.

Five tips for marketing your podcast

After creating your podcast and making it available to the masses for download, there is no guarantee that a ton of people will download or subscribe to your podcast. Unless you market yourself and your podcast episodes. Most podcasters are always searching for easy and free ways to market their episodes. Here are a few tips to get you started.

Tip One: Use social media, creatively

Market yourself and your podcasts through the various social media platforms available today. In my opinion and experience, social media has made it easy to generate tons of followers and fans. Depending on the nature of your podcasts, you can opt to use Facebook or Twitter, the two biggest social media platforms. Each has its own advantages and disadvantages. So choose according to your needs.

Tip Two: Use contests to drum up conversations about the podcast

Contests are an ingenious way of revving up conversations on any topic. You can ask your fans or followers trivia questions on social media and offer your podcast to the first person who gets the correct answer first. This not only gets the conversation, download, and subscribers trickling in, it also guarantees you a loyal following.

Tip Three: Befriend other podcasters

While they may be your competition, they are also the best way to drive up traffic and subscribers to your podcast.

Additionally, you get some new friends along the way. Who hates making new friends? Podcasters love giving each other shootouts and inviting other podcasters to cohost their shows. Cohost someone else's show and you are also drumming up some loyal followers from their show. This amounts to free marketing.

Tip Four: Promote for other shows

If you have invested in some podcasting equipment, there is no reason why you should let that equipment rust away while you are not using it. Ask your podcaster friends if you can create promos for them. Sweepers or promos are about 10-15 seconds each and go something like this

"Hello, this is {your name} from {you podcast name} and you are listening to {the name of the host/s} at {the name of their podcast}."

While this may seem like a total waste of your time and talent, the potential is great. Think about the number of clips and times they may play that promo clip.

Tip Five: give interviews

With a thousand podcasts in production per week, it is not extremely hard to find a podcaster looking for a potential interviewee. Depending on your podcast subject, you can have a wide pool of interviews to choose. Great places to find interview opportunities are HARO and RadioGuestList.com.

With your podcast live, and a few thousand loyal subscribers under your wing, it is now time to think about monetizing your podcast and make some serious cash from your podcasting efforts. The next chapter will cover exactly that.

Monetizing Your Podcasting Efforts

Making money from your podcast should not be your main motivation. However, making some money from something you love and enjoy doing is always an added advantage. There are many ways to monetize your podcast. In fact, there is no correct or wrong way to monetize your podcast. However, you have to ensure that no matter which method you opt for, it is something your audience would be comfortable with or love to try. Here are a few tips you can use to monetize your podcast.

Sell your podcast

This is the simplest and most straightforward way to monetizing your podcast. However, it is important to point out that most podcasts are free and a pay-per-listen podcast competes with many free podcasts. Nevertheless, if you feel like you have some real and valuable if not precious advice in your podcast, you can sell it by setting up a web store and charging subscribers per episode.

Sell advertising space

You can sell advertising space on your podcast by inserting short commercial in between your podcast sessions. A very neat option to selling advertising space is to get sponsorship for the podcast. For example, rather than play an interlude song, you can play a sponsored ad for that period. The trick to advertising is to ensure that the adverts you give space to are relevant to your podcast. Further, do not overdo the advertisements by adding too many commercials to the podcast.

Try web advertising

Each time you add a new podcast, the user device automatically downloads it. This makes it a bit difficult to offer advertisement. However, with a little effort and ingenuity, it is a possibility. You can try the podcast to a blog or website and mention the blog or website frequently in your podcast. This will drive some traffic to your website and earn you some AdSense revenue. The traffic from the podcast is a gold mine. You can place banner and sidebar ads.

Conclusion

Despite everything we have learnt, podcasting has no real roadmap. The only way to get better at it is to get going, practice and create as many podcasts as you can. Further, if you fail to have some fun while podcasting, you will not stick to podcasting. Moreover, podcasting demands some patience and perseverance before success comes knocking on your door. Other than that, it is an exciting journey well worth trying.

About the Author

Sam Raiden is a long-term work-at-home advocate and Internet entrepreneur. He has been involved in online marketing in some capacity for nearly 20 years. In the last 15 years, he has created numerous products and services with an appeal to a wide variety of audiences.

From ClickBank products to YouTube videos to blogs and podcasting, Sam has been obsessed with learning, using, and sharing the nuances of Internet marketing and how to generate streams of passive income from home.

Thank You

I'd also like to take a moment to thank you for picking up my book. I very much hope you enjoyed this work as much as I enjoyed creating it.

I'd love to ask a favor of you. If you liked the book, would you be kind enough to leave a vote and a review on Amazon? Doing so would help me greatly and will help support the creation of other books on this and similar topics.

www.ingramcontent.com/pod-product-compliance
Lightning Source LLC
Chambersburg PA
CBHW071019180526
45168CB00003B/1480